Bruce Tulgan's

JUSTinTIME Leadership

*Managing
the Free Agent
Workforce*

HRD PRESS
Amherst, Massachusetts

Published by: HRD Press, Inc.
                22 Amherst Road
                Amherst, MA 01002
                800-822-2801 (U.S. and Canada)
                413-253-3488
                413-253-3490 (fax)
                http://www.hrdpress.com

ISBN: 0-87425-573-2

Cover design by Eileen Klockars
Editorial and production services by Mary George

֍ Dedication

*To **Frances Coates Applegate,** my youngest niece, who, whether sitting on my lap, on the floor, on my desk, or in her "exer-saucer" workstation, was my good and diligent muse during the writing of this book.*

Contents

≡ **ACKNOWLEDGMENTS** ≡

AS ALWAYS, I must thank first and foremost the many thousands of incredible people who have shared with us over the years the lessons of their experiences in the workplace. Each interview has been a profound learning experience, and I am grateful to every single one of you who took the time to share your voice. Without your insights, there would be no Rainmaker-Thinking.

I am also indebted to all of the business leaders and managers who have expressed so much confidence in our work, and who gave me the opportunity to learn from the management issues they must deal with and solve on a daily basis. Thank you for all that you have taught me and for the chance to work with such fine people. I am honored by your faith and thrilled to be included in your efforts to make your organizations even better than they are.

To the tens of thousands who have attended my seminars, I again say thanks for listening, for laughing, for sharing the wisdom of your experience, for pushing me with the really tough questions, for all of your kindness, and for continually teaching me.

I am ever grateful to Bob Carkhuff, my publisher, and his team at HRD Press (especially Mary George) for our close working relationship and their ongoing confidence in me and in our work at RainmakerThinking. Thank you, Bob and HRD Press. We couldn't ask for better partners in the training business.

To my colleagues at RainmakerThinking, especially Jeff Coombs, Mark Kurber, Tansy Birenbaum, Cobb Still, and Dr. Carolyn Martin, thank you for your hard work and commitment and for your valuable contributions to this enterprise every single day.

To my family and friends, deepest thanks for being you and for allowing me to be who I am. Thanks especially to my grandmother Gertrude Tulgan (one hundred years old at this writing); my parents, Henry and Norma Tulgan; my parents-in-law, Julie and Paul Applegate; my nieces, Elisa, Erin, Frances, and Perry; my nephew, Joey; my sisters, Ronna and Tanya; and my brothers, Jim, Shan, and Tom.

As always, I reserve my utmost special thanks for my wife, Debby Applegate, who is my best friend, my smartest friend, my most loving friend, my toughest friend, my partner in all things, half of my soul, owner of my heart, and the person without whom I would indeed be lost. Thanks, Debby.

INTRODUCTION

HOW DO YOU GET the best people to pay their dues and climb the ladder in the old-fashioned way? You don't. Not in the new economy. Today, like all leaders and managers, you must be lean and flexible, maintain access to the talent you need, and maximize that talent on an as-needed basis. The JUSTinTIME Leadership pocket guide puts you on the course to meeting these requirements. It equips you with systems and practices designed to help leaders and managers get *the best work* out of *the best people* on a *consistent basis—wherever, whenever, and however those people can add value.*

JUSTinTIME Leadership is a highly innovative approach to management founded on extensive, timely research conducted by RainmakerThinking. This foundation has been shaped by our work with thousands of managers in hundreds of different organizations since the mid 1990s, and is informed by our ongoing workplace-interview research as well.

The basic assumption of JUSTinTIME Leadership is quite simple:The new economy will increasingly demand that companies move beyond static long-term

staffing models toward a more fluid model; in response, most successful companies will organize
themselves around small core groups of longer-term
employees and rely on large fluid talent pools. For
managers, this will mean drawing on the fluid talent
pools *as needed* to staff projects, tasks, and responsibilities; consequently, a whole range of management
practices will undergo fundamental changes.

JUSTinTIME Leadership gives leaders and managers a running start on these changes. The practices
it outlines are *best practices* for getting the advantage
by maximizing human talent in the unpredictable,
high-speed, high-tech, knowledge-driven, fiercely
competitive, new global economy.

The many benefits of employing these JUSTinTIME
practices include the following:

- Human resources that grow at desired levels
  without compromising productivity

- An improved return on recruiting and training
  investments

- The ability to seize, first and fast, the
  opportunities of the new market as they
  emerge

- A dynamic corporate culture that promotes
  innovation

The best practices cover six leadership areas, which are detailed in the overview below and form the main body of this pocket guide.

A Brief Overview of the Pocket Guide

Chapter 1 presents a fuller discussion of the new economy and JUSTinTIME Leadership, including a section on the new "free agent" career path.

Chapters 2 through 7 each focus on a series of best practices in a particular leadership area:

➡ **Staffing:** How to rethink the role of your core group and thrive on a fluid talent pool.

➡ **Training:** How to get people up to speed quickly, keep them learning on an as-needed basis, and make each one a "knowledge worker."

➡ **Performance management:** How to manage results instead of time, assemble the best teams, delegate to individuals effectively, and help contributors manage their work and time; also, how to evaluate performance in a manner that is brief, straightforward, and simple.

➡ **Coaching:** How to turn supervisory managers into day-to-day performance coaches.

➡️ **Rewards and incentives:** How to increase the ratio of performance-based rewards, adjust the timing of rewards, and customize rewards to achieve maximum incentive value; also, how to position managers as purchasing agents in relation to the results of individual contributors.

➡️ **Retention:** How to transform the meaning of retention, make personal retention plans with the most valuable contributors, and transform the reasons why people leave into the reasons why people stay.

Chapter 8 concludes the pocket guide with a quick and handy JUSTinTIME review.

This material includes concrete action steps and helpful brainstorming exercises, along with worksheets for applying the action steps and generated ideas to the issues you are facing in your organization or team.

THE CALL FOR JUSTinTIME LEADERSHIP

I have already shared the JUSTinTIME Leadership approach with thousands of business leaders, both in speeches all over the world and in my work with clients. The response? Overwhelmingly positive. In fact, so many leaders have asked for more JUSTin-

TIME Leadership resources that I have developed a management training program to accompany this pocket guide. *The JUSTinTIME Leadership Seminar* is designed to help you teach managers the best practices for managing the free-agent workforce in the new economy, and joins our growing line of books and training programs published by HRD Press.

A FINAL NOTE

As you read the following chapters, please remember that, while many of the best practices are about policies that cannot be made on the front lines, most of them can be applied, at least in part, without big changes in company policy. When you start doing things differently in your sphere of control, and your team shows dramatic improvements in productivity, morale, and retention, other people in the organization will take notice. That's when your actions will be recognized as signs of bold and innovative leadership. Ultimately, it is the bold actions of managers who are willing to take risks and create pockets of change that lead to wholesale changes in company policy.

I wish you the best of luck in becoming a change leader, wherever these words find you working.

1.

JUSTinTIME Leadership

"JUSTinTIME Leadership" sounds like a contradiction in terms, right? Leadership should be well planned, patient, and enduring. *Sorry.* There's no time for that anymore. Organizations are in constant flux, and individuals are in constant motion. The business mantra of the new economy is *"just-in-time"*—just-in-time design, sourcing, production, distribution, inventory. We've reached the point where we need to bring leadership practices into alignment.

In essence, leadership has always been about bringing out the best in people. And that will never change. But bringing out the best in people in the new just-in-time workplace requires a fundamental shift in management competencies.

THE NEW MODEL OF WORK

We are living through the most profound changes in the economy since the Industrial Revolution. Technology, globalization, and the accelerating pace of change have yielded chaotic markets, fierce competition, and unpredictable staffing needs.

In the late 1980s, business leaders and managers began responding to these factors by seeking much greater organizational flexibility. Reengineering increased speed and efficiency with improved systems and technology. Before long, companies in every industry were redesigning almost everything about the way work gets done. Work systems, some of which had been in place for decades, were dismantled and refashioned to improve flexibility, efficiency, and effectiveness.

As businesses reinvented work processes, they also eliminated layers of management, making way for today's fluid cross-trained teams, which tackle whatever work needs to be done whenever it needs to be done. Downsizing and restructuring made organizations leaner and more elastic by expanding their range of staffing options; instead of having to rely solely on full-time, long-term employees, companies could also draw on temps, independent contractors, part-timers, and the like—and so staff up or down on an *as-needed* basis. That's why the fastest growing forms of work over the last ten years have been temporary work, leased work, outsourced work, consulting, and small to mid-size business entrepreneurship (fueled largely by the booms in temping, leasing, outsourcing, and consulting). Each of these forms of work lends flexibility to employment relationships.

In a relatively brief span of time, then, organizational response to the new economy virtually freed work from the confines of the old-fashioned job and its rigid protocol: going to work every day at the same company in the same building during the same hours to do the same tasks in the same position with the same responsibility in the same chain of command, and thereby paying your dues and climbing "the ladder of success." Now the rule of thumb is, get the work done—whenever you can, wherever you can, however you can—whatever the work may be on any given day.

Because of this fundamental reshaping of the nature of work, organizations are more nimble than ever before and much better able to compete in today's high-tech, fast-paced, knowledge-driven global economy. The relationship between employers and employees has been altered radically and irrevocably.

THE NEW "FREE AGENT" CAREER PATH

Business leaders killed the old model for success—the dues-paying career path defined by long-term employment and corporate loyalty—because the new economy began calling for a whole new relationship between employers and employees. However, few of those leaders predicted that the workers with the most marketable skills, and consistently in greatest demand, would find they could do better by fending for themselves than they ever had by following the old career path. Still, that's exactly what happened. And now a whole new career path is emerging.

Many workers, especially the best educated and most skilled, see themselves as sole proprietors of their skills and abilities—as "free agents." These free agents think of their employers as "clients," and tend to juggle several clients at a time. They appear to move seamlessly from one new opportunity to the next—soaking up training resources, building relationships with decision-makers, and collecting proof of their ability to add value—and cash out their career investments on a regular basis, usually so they can reassess and renegotiate.

To the free agent, success is not defined by where one stands in relation to the hierarchy of a particular organization. What matters is one's ability to add value and to sell that value on the open market. Every untapped resource is waiting to be mined. Every unmet need is an opportunity to add value. Every person is a potential customer.

Today free agency is sweeping across the workforce like wildfire. More and more people are realizing they can keep doing what they know how to do well, and earn good money at it, without holding a permanent job or even a job per se. In the new economy, it's not the employer in the driver's seat, but the individual. The skills that make you valuable to an employer belong to you and nobody else; when you leave your employer, those skills and your ability to add value leave with you—they go wherever you go. And there are places *to* go. Security is not found in stability and commitments, but in mobility and options.

Suddenly, fewer and fewer skilled people are clinging to their jobs and crying, "Don't downsize me!" The balance of power in the labor market has shifted.

BUSINESS AND THE PERPETUAL STAFFING CRISIS

In today's fast-paced, fiercely competitive business environment, experience and seniority no longer rule the job market. Instead, a new breed of talent is in high demand: individuals who are adaptable, independent, technoliterate, information-savvy, and entrepreneurial. Every organization in every industry today is spending more time, more energy, and more money than ever before to recruit such talent. But the supply of skilled workers is simply not growing fast enough, at any level, to meet organizational needs.

If you ask business leaders and managers everyday, as I do, they will tell you that the most pressing and seemingly unsolvable problem facing them today is employee turnover. And the problem is not only that turnover is increasing, but that it is also changing. The best people used to be the ones most likely to stay in the firm, pay their dues, and climb the ladder; but more and more, they are the ones most apt to leave. Why? Because they *can* leave. And while employers have human resources teams working double-time to solve the problem, it just keeps getting worse.

Perhaps the most troubling news is that the staffing crisis is likely to continue for the foreseeable future. More and more work in all segments of the economy requires more and more skill. Largely for that reason, the demand for skilled workers will keep growing faster than the supply.

Skilled employees are in such great demand, and employers so concerned about retaining them and getting a decent return on their recruiting and training investment, that employees have more negotiating power in the workplace than ever before. In this climate, employers can no longer expect employees to be motivated by prospects of long-term employment, advancement up an organization's hierarchy, annual raises, and other rewards and incentives from the workplace of the past.

What does this mean for business? That employers cannot go back to promising job security in exchange for loyalty—they need to stay lean and flexible in the post-industrial age, even while they are scrambling for access to the best talent.

JUSTinTIME Leadership

The best way for employers to adapt to the conditions of the new economy is to embrace free agency as the natural consequence of reengineering, restructuring, and downsizing, and to realize that free agency is a perfect fit with the needs of the new nimble organization. Stop trying to hold back the tide. Jump in and learn how to swim!

JUSTinTIME Leadership is about retooling expectations and competencies so that everything is done on an *as-needed* basis. That way organizations can thrive on short-term flexible employment relationships with the best free-agent employees, utilizing their talents when those talents are needed. Most of the necessary changes are well under way. But employers still need to adjust their expectations about the employer-employee relationship and transform their practices and systems for managing people to fit the new relationship.

The assumptions of JUSTinTIME Leadership, stated earlier in this pocket guide's introduction, are well founded and cannot be ignored. In the new economy, organizations will indeed have to move beyond the static long-term staffing model and toward a more fluid model. The most successful companies will in fact organize around small core groups of longer-term employees, and they will rely increasingly on large fluid talent pools. Managers will draw on these fluid pools on an as-needed basis when it comes time to staff projects, tasks, and responsibilities. And management practices will indeed change in fundamental ways.

In these more flexible organizations, the most important ability of a manager will be to get the best work out of the best people consistently—wherever, whenever, and however the best people can contribute the most work at the highest levels of speed and accuracy. Flexible work arrangements will no longer be the exceptions, but the norm. While most employment engagements will be short-term, the most valuable contributors will return to the best employers regularly to take on new assignments—when they are needed, and as long as they are available. And because these valuable contributors will likely be juggling several clients and projects at the same time, managers will have to learn how to share talent.

The fluid staffing model will thus require changes in many systems and competencies. JUSTinTIME

Leadership offers leaders and managers a set of guidelines and processes for making the necessary adjustments. Let's a take a closer look, beginning with JUSTinTIME staffing.

2.

JUST in TIME
Staffing

UNTIL RECENTLY, the dominant staffing model for most employers was based on long-term employment relationships with long-term employees. People were expected to start in entry-level positions appropriate to their skills and credentials, and then, over time, move their way up the ladder. The key features of this model were stability and predictability. Staffing strategy was all about planning for openings in an otherwise static organization chart. With slight adjustments, the positions on the chart remained the same, like the positions on a sports team; only the people who filled those positions would change periodically, like the players on a sports team.

But in today's quickly changing marketplace, where employers can never predict what is just around the corner, the old-fashioned, stable, long-term employer-employee relationship just doesn't fit. Now the key to continued organizational success is the ability to adapt rapidly to new circumstances, whether they are unexpected market opportunities or suddenly vanishing market opportunities. Depending on the immediate situation, staffing may have to expand or contract, or expand in one area while contracting in another—and do so rapidly. Certain skills suddenly may be required, and others, just as suddenly, may no longer be necessary. In the new economy, staffing needs will be in constant flux. Employers must gear their staffing strategies toward coping with this reality.

To meet unpredictable staffing needs on an as-needed basis, employers must move toward a more fluid staffing model. Again, most already have done so by utilizing temps, independent contractors, outsourcing, and so on. But their organization charts do not reflect it, nor do their expectations about relationships with their employees, nor do their management practices and rewards systems. These must all be adjusted.

The following JUSTinTime best practices provide concrete action steps that will help you successfully make the transition to a more fluid staffing model. Brainstorming exercises have been included, as well as two new-staff planning worksheets for putting your exercise results into a highly usable form.

JUSTinTIME Best Practices
— Staffing —

1. Shrink your core group, and retool your organization so it can thrive with a very small number of full-time, long-term, on-site employees. The goal is to maintain a coherent core group of leaders (agenda-setters) and facilitators (those who delegate and monitor results).

The best strategy is to build powerful incentives— equity or at least a stake in the bottom line—to retain key core groupers as long as possible. Recognize that there will be relatively few long-termers even among the core group, and that a portion of any core group will turn over regularly.

2. Grow your fluid talent pool. Reorganize as much day-to-day work as possible so it can be done by that pool's talent—short-term employees working in flexible arrangements, employees who leave and then return on a fairly regular basis, temporary employees, independent contractors—and through outsourcing.

3. Build a proprietary talent database of individual contributors whom you can call upon for temporary help as needed. Index the database by key skill and performance criteria, and train core groupers to staff as much work as possible from this talent pool. Draw from a wide range of sources, including your existing employees, former employees, and those who receive but do not accept employment offers from you.

Build your database on an ongoing basis by attracting a steady stream of potential applicants. Screen applicants in or out of your talent database using an appropriate selection process (on-line interviews and tests, submission of prior work products, letters of reference, and so on). Draw on the database as needed to staff projects, tasks, and responsibilities.

Ultimately, the most valuable people in your fluid talent pool will be those who develop track records of working effectively with your organization. Of course, some people may move back and forth between your fluid talent pool and your core group.

 Develop solid working relationships with a wide range of vendors who can be counted upon for outsourcing. Identify potential vendors in every area of work that the organization needs to tackle.

As often as possible, use vendors for limited assignments when the need for them is not urgent; this will allow you to evaluate them on a trial basis. Keep complete records of the capabilities of each vendor, and seek to establish priority customer status with the best vendors.

5. Maintain an internal group of contributors who are not permanently assigned to any particular tasks/responsibilities, teams, locations, or schedules, and who can be called upon and deployed to fill in staffing gaps wherever and whenever they occur. Individuals best suited to this group will be those who are both diversely skilled and who prefer variable working conditions.

Initiate these best practices with the JUSTinTIME brainstorming exercises and planning worksheets for staffing.

Use the two handy worksheets that conclude this chapter to shape your brainstorming results into useful plans that will answer your staffing needs.

↳

Brainstorming
Exercises — Staffing

A. STAFFING EVALUATION

Purpose: To evaluate your current staffing situation.

❶ List the key players in your organization (or team).

❷ For each key player, answer the following questions:

  1. What is this person's title or official position on the organization chart?

    Does the title/position fit the person's actual role? Are there others with the same title/position who have very different roles?

  2. What does this person actually do? What are his or her tasks and responsibilities?

    Which of these tasks and responsibilities are fixed and which change periodically?

  3. How long has this person been part of your organization (or team)?

    How has this person's role evolved over time?

  4. What would happen if this person left your organization (or team)?

→ *Brainstorming Exercises*

What work would not get done right away? What work would not get done over the course of a week? A month? Would you need to replace the person? How many of his or her tasks and responsibilities could be reassigned or eliminated?

5. Is this person part of your core group? Should this person be part of that group?

B. WORK INVENTORY

Purpose: To inventory the work that currently needs doing in your organization.

❶ Make a list of the results that must be achieved by your organization (or team).

❷ For each result, answer the following questions:

1. What concrete actions must be accomplished to drive this result forward?

Can these actions be separated and carried out by different people? If so, which ones? Are there several concrete actions that should or must be done in concert by the same person?

2. How often are these concrete actions performed? Are they done every day?

➡ *Brainstorming Exercises*

Several times a week? Less frequently?

3. Are these concrete actions fixed, or do they change from time to time?

4. How much skill, knowledge, and/or experience is required to enable a person to accomplish these concrete actions?

   Is a great deal of training necessary? Or could these actions be accomplished without much training?

5. Which of these actions should be done by a person who is part of your core group?

6. Which of these actions could be done by people working in more flexible arrangements (e.g., temps, independent contractors, flex-timers) or through outsourcing?

C. STRATEGY PLANNING
Purpose: To plan your staffing strategy as if you were starting from scratch.

What results does your organization (or team) need to achieve? What work must you get done?

❶ The Core Group
How many people do you need in your core group? Who do you want to have in the group?

➤ *Brainstorming Exercises*

List the individuals by name (or by role if you don't have a particular person in mind). For each person in your core group, answer the following questions:

1. What role do you envision for this person?

2. What tasks and responsibilities do you want this person to assume?

   How much of this work is relatively fixed? How much is changing from time to time?

3. What skills, knowledge, and experience will this person need?

   Will the person require any training to prepare for the role?

4. Do you need this person to be full-time?

5. Do you need this person to be on-site?

6. Do you need this person to be exclusive (that is, to work only for your organization or team)?

7. Do you need this person to work for you on an uninterrupted basis (that is, not to leave and return)?

   For how long must his or her service remain uninterrupted?

→ *Brainstorming Exercises*

8. What kind of decision-making authority will this person have?

❷ The Fluid Talent Pool

First, please consider the following two questions:

- How many people do you need in your fluid talent pool?

- What work can be done effectively by people working in more flexible employment relationships with the organization (or team)?

Now answer the questions below:

1. What tasks and responsibilities could be done effectively by temporary employees on an as-needed basis?

List all the individuals you can think of who could be included in a proprietary talent database (for example, former employees).

2. What tasks and responsibilities could be handled effectively by independent contractors or other outside sources on an as-needed basis?

➤ *Brainstorming Exercises*

> *List all the individuals and independent vendors you can think of who could be included in a group of outside sources and called upon on an outsourcing basis.*

3. What tasks and responsibilities could be handled effectively by internal contributors who are not permanently assigned, but work in more flexible arrangements?

> *List all the individuals you can think of who might be good candidates for more flexible internal work arrangements.*

CONCLUDED

Use your brainstorming results to begin planning with the following worksheets.

WORKSHEET: NEW STAFF PLANNING (A)

Directions: Record the results to be achieved, the concrete action steps for achieving them, and the staffing option and individual(s) most suitable for fulfilling each step.

Results	Concrete Actions	Staffing Option 1.Core 2.Temp 3.Independent 4.Internal Flex	Individual

➜ WORKSHEET: PLANNING (A)

Individual	
Staffing Option 1.Core 2.Temp 3.Independent 4.Internal Flex	
Concrete Actions	
Results	

WORKSHEET: NEW STAFF PLANNING (B)

Directions: List individuals and their tasks according to staffing position—core group, temporary, independent, or internal flex.

Core Group		Temporary		Independent		Internal Flex	
Individuals	Tasks	Individual	Tasks	Individual	Tasks	Individual	Tasks

→ WORKSHEET: PLANNING (B)

Internal Flex	Tasks	
	Individual	
Independent	Tasks	
	Individual	
Temporary	Tasks	
	Individual	
Core Group	Tasks	
	Individuals	

3.

JUSTinTIME
Training

ORGANIZATIONS IN ALL INDUSTRIES are investing more in employee training and development than ever before. That's because highly skilled and knowledgeable employees are critical to an organization's competitive position in the new economy. Value adding, problem solving, and innovation are the winning elements in today's marketplace. Those elements require *smart* work every bit as much as, if not more than, they require hard work. Thus it is absolutely necessary for companies to train their employees all the way from the corner office to the factory floor, and then train them some more.

CONTINUOUS LEARNING, CONTINUOUS TRAINING

The need for smart, well-trained employees is nothing new—throughout the industrial era, such workers were a key to organizational advantage. But efficiency, quantity, and uniformity were more important daily goals for most workers than value adding, problem solving, and innovation. And although most employees required plenty of training, very few had to be trained every day from the first day to the last day of their working lives. To be sure, people did a substantial amount of their career learning on the job, developing and refining their formal education and initial training through practical application in the real world. However, it was widely assumed that most people completed the bulk of their education in formal schooling, before embarking on their working lives.

Not anymore.

Continuous learning is now the job of every person throughout every organization, and ensuring that continuous learning is taking place is a critical goal of every business leader and manager. The problem is, today's information environment produces more information in a single day than an army of people could master in a lifetime; so organizations have to devote more and more resources just to keep up with the flow of new information. Basic knowledge and skills routinely become obsolete and must be replaced with up-to-date knowledge and new skills. Continuous learning has come to mean continuous training. This is why employers are investing so much in training. Quite simply, they must.

But do they get big returns on that investment? Not necessarily.

THE TRAINING INVESTMENT PARADOX— AND SOLUTION

Ironically, the more companies train their employees, the more marketable those employees become—and the more likely they are to leave the organization for a better offer. I call this "the training investment paradox." Employers simply do not get the return they need on their training investment when their employees turn over too soon, especially when their employees go to work for the competition, which then gets the investment return.

This is one reason why organizations need to adopt more flexible employment relationships, for the more ways an organization has of employing a person, the more ways it has of getting a return on the training invested in that person. Once the organization has made that training investment, it has a strong interest in continuing to get work out of the person, even if it's not in a traditional employment arrangement. As long as the employee continues to work—whether full-time, part-time, on flex-time, via telecommuting, or what have you—the organization can continue reaping a return on its training investment. Indeed, organizations that are able to manage more fluid employment relationships will not only get more out of their training investments but also find themselves reaping windfall dividends from the training investments of other, less flexible employers.

Of course, flexible employment relationships are not enough to solve the training investment paradox. Fundamental adjustments must also be made in training practices themselves.

Organizations need to stop training their employees for the long haul—that approach was based on the assumptions of the old-fashioned, long-term career path. It makes much more sense to train people only on an as-needed basis—to take the JUSTinTIME approach. By investing in just-in-time learning resources, organizations can separate a large part of their return on investment from the employment duration of individual employees. Moreover, just-in-time training allows learners to select the precise information required to fill skill and knowledge gaps as those gaps occur; thus, it is in sync with the learning needs of individuals in today's information environment.

The JUSTinTIME approach to training is encapsulated in the best practices below. The brainstorming exercise and planning worksheets that follow them will get you started on putting these practices into action.

JUSTinTIME Best Practices
— Training —

1. Train people one step at a time, instead of training them for the long term. Gear the training of individual contributors to the specific tasks, responsibilities, and projects on which they will be working in the very near term.

2. Put new contributors through your own "boot camp." Get them up to speed quickly so they can start adding value right away.

3. Create a just-in-time training infrastructure that can support ongoing, as-needed learning. Provide maximum information resources in different media, and give learners the remote control. Look ahead, and try to anticipate the learning needs that may emerge, the skill and knowledge gaps that may develop, the refreshers that may be useful, and any information that may come in handy. Also, prepare contributors to anticipate their own needs. Gear just-in-time learning resources to anticipated gaps.

4. Transform your corporate culture by making everyone *a knowledge worker.* Knowledge work is not about what you do, but about how you do it. If a contributor goes out of his

or her way to leverage information resources, and
employs skill and knowledge to accomplish tasks
and meet responsibilities, then however basic the
tasks and responsibilities, that contributor is a knowledge worker.

Help every single contributor identify information resources and make plans for leveraging skill and
knowledge to accomplish every task and meet every
responsibility, no matter how basic.

***Initiate these best practices with
the JUSTinTIME brainstorming exercise
and planning worksheets for training.***

Use the three worksheets that conclude this
chapter to plan for up-to-speed training,
as-needed learning, and knowledge work, to
address your training needs.

$\hookrightarrow$

Brainstorming
Exercise — Training

TRAINING EVALUATION

Purpose: To evaluate your current training situation.

❶ Please answer the following questions:

1. What is the average investment made in training individual contributors?

2. How do you evaluate the return you are getting on that investment?

3. What is the overall approach to training in your organization (or team)?

- Train for the long term?
- Or one step at a time?

4. How quickly do you get new contributors up to speed?

- Immediately?
- Several weeks?
- Several months?

5. What is the overall approach to continuous learning?

- Mostly classroom-based learning at scheduled intervals?
- Or as-needed by remote control?

➤ *Brainstorming Exercise*

6. Who are the teachers in your organization?

   • Members of the training team?
   • Some of the better managers who take the time to help workers?
   • Everybody?

7. In your organization, which contributors are treated like knowledge workers?

   • Nobody?
   • Certain people with high-level tasks?
   • Everybody?

8. What learning resources are currently available to individual contributors?

❷ Now make a list of all the learning resources that could be made available to individual contributors.

Brainstorm innovative ways to make these resources available.

CONCLUDED

Now begin your
JUSTinTIME training planning
with the following worksheets.

WORKSHEET: UP-TO-SPEED TRAINING

Directions: Select a contributor or category of contributors with a particular role and established tasks and responsibilities.

1. List the results that each contributor must achieve in the immediate future.

2. For each result, what concrete actions will the contributor have to accomplish?

3. For each concrete action, what knowledge is required? What skill? What wisdom? What experience?

4. What is the fastest and most effective way to bring the contributor up to speed on this knowledge, skill, wisdom, and experience?

QUICK UP-TO-SPEED TRAINING PLANNER

Contributor: _____

Results	Concrete Actions	Required Knowledge, Skill, Wisdom, Experience	Fastest Effective Way to Bring Contributor Up to Speed

➔ **WORKSHEET: TRAINING**

QUICK UP-TO-SPEED TRAINING PLANNER

Results	Concrete Actions	Required Knowledge, Skill, Wisdom, Experience	Fastest Effective Way to Bring Contributor Up to Speed

WORKSHEET: AS-NEEDED LEARNING

Directions: Select a contributor or category of contributors with a particular role and established tasks and responsibilities.

1. List the contributor's key tasks and responsibilities (that is, the results that must be achieved and the corresponding concrete actions that must be accomplished).

2. For each task and responsibility, anticipate the skill and knowledge gaps the contributor is likely to encounter in doing the work. For instance, what are the likely problems, challenges, roadblocks, wildcards? What questions does a relatively new person in this position commonly ask?

   As you anticipate and identify these likely gaps, list them.

3. For each anticipated gap, answer these questions:

   ■ What are the best available learning resources the contributor could tap into as needed, when the gap occurs?

   ■ Are there learning resources not currently available that could be made available?

   ■ Is there a simple way to create guideposts in these resources to match up appropriate information with the gaps? (For example, a list of answers to the questions commonly asked.)

4. What is the best way to make these learning resources available to individual contributors on an as-needed basis?

Be sure to record your answers on the
AS-NEEDED LEARNING PLANNER

→ WORKSHEET: LEARNING

AS-NEEDED LEARNING PLANNER

Contributor: _____

Tasks and Responsibilities	Anticipated Skill and Knowledge Gaps	Learning Resources to Fill Anticipated Gaps	Plan for Making Resources Available on As-Needed Basis

→ WORKSHEET: LEARNING

Tasks and Responsibilities	Anticipated Skill and Knowledge Gaps	Learning Resources to Fill Anticipated Gaps	Plan for Making Resources Available on As-Needed Basis

WORKSHEET: KNOWLEDGE WORK

Directions: Select a contributor or category of contributors with a particular role and established tasks and responsibilities.

1. List the contributor's key tasks and responsibilities (that is, the results that must be achieved and the corresponding concrete actions that must be accomplished).

2. For each task and responsibility, *what* information resources could the contributor leverage to employ greater skill and knowledge in accomplishing this work?

   List the information resources and the corresponding skill or knowledge.

3. For each task and responsibility, *how* could the contributor leverage the information resource you've identified to employ greater skill or knowledge in accomplishing the work?

KNOWLEDGE WORK PLANNER

Contributor: _____

Tasks and Responsibilities	Information Resources That Can Be Leveraged	Opportunities to Employ Greater Skill and Knowledge	Plan for Using Resources to Employ This Skill and Knowledge

➔ WORKSHEET: KNOWLEDGE WORK

KNOWLEDGE WORK PLANNER

Tasks and Responsibilities	Information Resources That Can Be Leveraged	Opportunities to Employ Greater Skill and Knowledge	Plan for Using Resources to Employ This Skill and Knowledge

4.

JUST in TIME Performance Management

EMPOWERMENT WAS A BIG TOPIC among management thinkers in the 1990s because it had become a business imperative—the key to productivity as well as quality. However, productivity and quality are not the only reasons to empower individuals in today's new workplace: speed is another critical factor. To succeed in our fast-paced business world, organizations must be able to seize market opportunities before they disappear, consistently beat the competition to the marketplace, and achieve rapid turnaround rates on products and services.

The irony is that by focusing on time, managers tend to slow things down—the focus on hours worked almost always undermines the productivity of individual contributors. Managing time instead of performance is the biggest impediment to empowering contributors to achieve results with speed, quality, and innovation.

THE KEY TO EMPOWERMENT

The key to empowerment is effective delegation—giving individual contributors ownership of tangible results. In the workplace of the past, delegation was not so dynamic. Usually managers would delegate to employees relatively fixed assortments of tasks and responsibilities. These would be known as "job descriptions." And people often became very protective of their own areas of work, claiming job descriptions as their turf. But the relatively fixed job descriptions of the static workplace are a thing of the past. Nowadays, everyone has the same job description: Get the work done as fast as you can, whatever the work may be on any given day.

In the JUSTinTIME workplace, managers must be able to integrate fluid talent quickly and effectively on an ongoing basis without disrupting work-in-progress. Consequently, the work of managers has shifted from primarily managing time to almost exclusively managing results.

Managers in the new economy need to be, more than anything else, "results facilitators." That means day-to-day delegation is now the primary work of managers. Effective delegation enables managers to spend more time mobilizing resources for individual contributors, monitoring progress, problem-solving, keeping individual contributors focused and motivated, and rewarding high performers.

But simply telling employees "We want you to treat this project like your own little business" is not enough to achieve delegation effective enough to create real empowerment. You cannot empower people without establishing the terrain on which they have power. That terrain needs to be composed of tangible goals accompanied by concrete deadlines and clear guidelines and parameters.

To bring out the very best in the very best people, managers must be clear on the answers to these three essential questions:

1. Which roles are being played by which people in pursuit of which missions?

2. Where does each employee's responsibility begin, and where does it end?

3. For what will each contributor be held accountable, and how will the contributor be held accountable?

Managers need to ensure, on an ongoing basis, that their best people are clear on the answers too.

The following best practices will put you on the path to JUSTinTIME performance management, and keep you moving on it. Five JUSTinTIME worksheets have been included after these best practices, to help you with ad-hoc best teams, effective delegation, contributors' self-management, performance evaluation, and flexible work arrangements.

JUSTinTIME Best Practices
_ Performance _
Management

1. Don't let old-fashioned departments masquerade as teams. Departments are static, whereas teams are dynamic. Pull together teams based on who has the skills to fill the roles necessary to achieve clear goals with concrete deadlines. Require teams to disband when their mission is completed.

2. Assign every tangible result to an owner, and make certain that every result-owner accepts 100 percent responsibility at the time of delegation. Attach a concrete deadline to every tangible result, regardless of its scope. And be sure to spell out all the parameters, guidelines, and specifications at the time that you assign the results and deadlines.

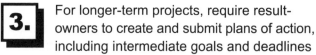

3. For longer-term projects, require result-owners to create and submit plans of action, including intermediate goals and deadlines along with the concrete action steps necessary to achieve each intermediate goal. Result-owners should report to managers on intermediate goals and deadlines as they occur, and should be prepared to adjust goals and fine-tune action plans as necessary.

4. Give the following advice to any individual contributor accepting ownership of tangible results:

No matter how small the results may be, you have 100 percent responsibility for them, and they are your proving ground. If you do a great job on the results, you will earn responsibility for greater and greater results.

To gain 100 percent ownership of any result, you must work closely with your manager from the very start of a project. Devote the time and energy it takes to get your manager to dissect projects to clearly delineate tangible results; then request 100 percent responsibility for at least one of these results. If your manager says, "That result is too much responsibility for you," what he or she really means is "This result is too big in scope for me to feel comfortable assigning you 100 percent responsibility for it." In such a case, get your manager to dissect the result and delineate even smaller results, until there is a result your manager feels comfortable assigning you. As you prove your ability to achieve results that are smaller and have close deadlines, you will earn responsibility for larger results, and you can work with your manager over time to set deadlines that correspond to the increasing scope of the larger results you will own.

Finally, whenever you accept ownership for tangible results, make, follow, and be accountable to an action plan.

5. Instead of relying on the old-fashioned, lengthy, six- and twelve-month performance evaluations, make performance evaluation about performance and nothing else. Keep it brief, straight, simple, and tied directly to measuring the achievement of goals and deadlines.

6. Manage *results* instead of time. As long as individual contributors are delivering results, forget about time altogether. Offer flexible work arrangements (such as compressed schedules, flex-time, telecommuting, part-time, job sharing, and sabbaticals) and support employees when they are in need of a morning stroll, a mid-day workout, an afternoon nap, a day off, or a vacation.

The best way to give individual contributors more flexible work arrangements is to go through the following process:

a. Inventory the person's tasks and responsibilities and projects.

b. Which ones need to be done in a particular building during certain hours?

c. Which ones don't?

d. When you find work that doesn't need to be done in a particular building during particular hours, you have found opportunities to give people more control over their schedules. Make those opportunities contingent on an ongoing track record of high performance.

> *Initiate these best practices with the JUSTinTIME worksheets for performance management.*

WORKSHEET: AD HOC BEST TEAMS

Directions: Follow the action steps below and record the information requested.

Remember: The components of a best team are *a clear mission* (goal, deadline, parameters) and *the right people with the right skills in the right roles.*

ACTION STEPS

1. Define the mission.

> ■ **Goal:**
>
> ■ **Deadline:**
>
> ■ **Guidelines & Parameters:**

2. Clarify the separate components of the mission.

MISSION COMPONENTS			
Results	Corresponding Roles	Necessary Skills	The Right Person
➡	➡	➡	
➡	➡	➡	↘

↱ WORKSHEET: AD HOC TEAMS

Continue to clarify the separate components of the mission.

MISSION COMPONENTS

Results	Corresponding Roles	Necessary Skills	The Right Person
➡	➡	➡	
➡	➡	➡	
➡	➡	➡	
➡	➡	➡	
➡	➡	➡	
➡	➡	➡	
➡	➡	➡	

WORKSHEET: EFFECTIVE DELEGATION

Directions: Use this tool as an aid to effective delegation.

Remember:

■ Assign every tangible result to an owner, and ensure every result-owner accepts 100 percent responsibility at the time of delegation.

■ Attach a deadline to every tangible result, large or small.

■ Spell out all the parameters, guidelines, and specifications at the time that results and deadlines are assigned.

ACTION STEPS AND CHARTS

1. Dissect every big result into a series of smaller results that are clearly delineated and tangible.

Big Result	Smaller Tangible Result	Smaller Tangible Result	Smaller Tangible Result	Smaller Tangible Result	Smaller Tangible Result

→ WORKSHEET: DELEGATION

2. Make sure each tangible result has an owner, and that the owner has 100 percent responsibility for that result.

Tangible Result	Owner

3. For each tangible result, establish up front a concrete deadline as well as clear guidelines and parameters.

Result	Deadline	Guidelines & Parameters

↱ **WORKSHEET:** DELEGATION

4. This process yields a matrix of results accompanied by owners, deadlines, guidelines, and parameters. Use the following chart to record your matrix of results.

RESULTS MATRIX			
Result	**Owner**	**Deadline**	**Guidelines & Parameters**

WORKSHEET: CONTRIBUTOR'S SELF-MANAGEMENT

Directions to Managers: This tool will help you support the self-management of contributors, which is especially important with longer-term projects. Require individual contributors to make, submit, follow, and be accountable for a basic plan of intermediate goals and deadlines. Give them a planner, such as the one below, that will guide them through this process.

CONTRIBUTOR'S RESULTS PLANNER

1. Make sure you have a clear picture of the tangible result you own, the concrete deadline for it, and all of its guidelines and parameters.

Tangible Result	Deadline	Guidelines & Parameters

2. For each larger result you own, set intermediate goals and corresponding intermediate deadlines.

   For example, if you have to send a packet of information out by 5 PM, what should you do by 4 PM? 3PM? 2PM? And so on. If you are going to deliver a report by June 1, what do you need to do by May 1? April 1? March 1?

→ WORKSHEET: SELF-MANAGEMENT

Use the chart below to schedule intermediate goals and
deadlines, and stay on track toward the results you own.

INTERMEDIATE DEADLINES AND RESULTS

Tangible Result	Intermediate Deadlines	Intermediate Results
Deadline		
Guidelines & Parameters		

3. Review your list of intermediate results and deadlines,
   and, using the next chart, break down each goal and
   deadline into concrete actions.

→ WORKSHEET: SELF-MANAGEMENT

CONCRETE ACTIONS		
Intermediate Deadline	*Intermediate Result*	*Concrete Actions*

Remember: Plugging concrete actions into your schedule every week is how you will turn your plan into results.

WORKSHEET: PERFORMANCE EVALUATION

Directions: Use the chart below to evaluate performance. Keep it brief, simple, and tied directly to measuring goal and deadline achievement. Remember, evaluate *performance* and nothing else.

Name:

	Achieved	Not Achieved		
Goal				
Deadline				
Guidelines & Parameters				

WORKSHEET: FLEXIBLE WORK ARRANGEMENTS

Directions: Select a contributor and, using the chart below, inventory his or her tasks and responsibilities. Determine which ones require working in a particular building during particular hours, and which ones don't. State your reasons, to be sure.

Name:

Tasks & Responsibilities	Certain Building? (Yes/No)	Certain Hours? (Yes/No)	Why? Are you sure?

➡ **WORKSHEET:** FLEXIBLE WORK

Tasks & Responsibilities	Certain Building? (Yes/No)	Certain Hours? (Yes/No)	Why? Are you sure?

Those tasks and responsibilities that don't have building/time requirements are opportunities to give people more control over their schedules. Make those opportunities contingent on an ongoing track record of high performance.

5.

JUSTinTIME
Coaching:
The FAST Feedback Method

SUPERVISORY MANAGERS in the new workplace must be performance-management coaches, and business leaders must hold every supervisory manager accountable for effectiveness in that role. According to our up-to-date research, the most important predictor of success—productivity, morale, and employment duration—for both long-term and short-term employees, as well as teams, is a coaching-style manager who knows how to give what we call *FAST Feedback.*

FAST Feedback is a system that encapsulates the best practices of the best coaching-style managers. Like our JUSTinTIME approach, this feedback system is based upon ongoing workplace-interview research conducted by RainmakerThinking (see sidebar, next page).

For more about FAST Feedback . . .

- **Want to learn more about the FAST method?**
- **Interested in teaching managers the key skills and best practices of this effective approach?**

If so, you're not alone. So many of our clients have asked for FAST resources that we at RainmakerThinking have developed a full-scale management training program called *FAST Feedback: Coaching Skills for Managers,* available from HRD Press. Also available is the second edition of *FAST Feedback,* a pocket guide that gives you the full basics along with many helpful exercises, worksheets, and practice tips.

For more information about these resources and our other programs and products from HRD Press, contact us at www.rainmakerthinking.com or give us a call at 203-772-2002.

FAST FEEDBACK

The fundamental principle of FAST Feedback is feedback itself. Feedback is different from other forms of communication because it is, by definition, a *responsive* form of communication. For example, feedback might be any of the following:

- An answer to a question
- The fulfillment of a request for information

Figure 1. Basic Feedback—A Response to Input

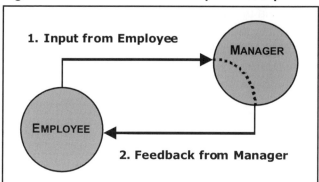

- A reply or rebuttal to a point
- A suggestion for revision of work
- The evaluation of performance

Managerial feedback allows contributors to gauge the success of their work performance. They need this kind of feedback for many reasons:

- To stay focused and motivated, and keep moving in the right direction

- To improve their performance

- To grow their spheres of individual responsibility without compromising quality

- To check on an ongoing basis what's changing and what's staying the same.

Feedback is fundamental to coaching because, by its very nature, coaching is an ongoing series of responses to the performance of whoever is being coached. Giving feedback is the core competency of every coach. Our research reveals that *the FASTer the feedback, the better the coach.*

THE **FAST** FORMULA

FAST is an acronym that stands for:

> ➡ **Frequent**
> ➡ **Accurate**
> ➡ **Specific**
> ➡ **Timely**

According to our research, these are the four elements employees most often ascribe to feedback from "the best manager [they've] ever had." These are also the four elements employees most often say they need *but don't get* in the feedback they receive from most managers.

Frequent. Some employees need feedback more often than others do—each one has his or her unique "feedback frequency." Giving each employee feedback at that unique rate of need is the first key behavior of the best coaching-style managers. *Identifying and "tuning in" to each employee's frequency* is the corresponding skill.

Accurate. Every instance of feedback affects trust and performance. Giving feedback that is correct, balanced, and appropriate is the second key behavior of effective coaching-style managers. *Taking time to reflect, question assumptions, check facts, and rehearse the feedback* is the second corresponding skill.

Specific. Telling people exactly what they do right and exactly what they do wrong is just not specific enough—you must also tell people exactly what you want them to do next. This is the third key behavior, with *setting concrete goals and deadlines, and providing clear guidelines,* as the corresponding skill.

Timely. The closer in time that feedback follows the performance in question, the more impact the feedback will have. Giving feedback immediately is thus the fourth key behavior of effective coaching-style managers. *Effective time management* is the corresponding skill.

The Need for Coaching With FAST Feedback

FAST Feedback is really about the day-to-day relationships between managers and the people they work with most closely—their direct reports and other valued co-workers.

Often the cause of ineffective management relation-ships is a lack of *consistent, focused attention and effort* on the manager's part. Many of those charged with managing people are so busy with other work that they neglect their supervisory responsibilities, such as up-front guidance, effective delegation, thorough revision of work in progress, detailed appraisal of fi-nal results, balanced feedback, and the rewarding of high performers. In effect, such managers wish their employees would simply manage themselves.

This neglect tends to result in mistakes and problems, even crises, that ultimately require the manager's at-tention *after all.* And when a manager is finally pulled away from scheduled tasks and responsibilities to intervene, he or she is likely to express displeasure with subordinates. Such expressions usually take the form of general reproach or instructions for damage control. Then the manager returns to business as usual, hoping employees will manage themselves until the next mistake, problem, or crisis —when the manager will be needed again . . . after all.

Too often the problem is one of skill. People are some-times promoted to supervisory positions because they are good at certain tasks or have departmental ex-perience, but not always because they are good at managing people. The result is that there are plenty of supervising managers out there who don't really know how to bring out the best in the people they supervise. When this is the case, employee morale, productivity, and retention all suffer immensely.

Day-to-day coaching-style management has always been an effective way to motivate employees, improve morale and productivity, and increase retention. But turning managers into performance coaches is *absolutely necessary* in today's fast-paced, rapidly changing JUSTinTIME workplace.

By practicing FAST Feedback, managers will find they are more able to:

- Provide contributors with regular guidance as they need it

- Give contributors a feeling of being "in the loop"

- Build credibility with contributors

- Enable more responsible delegation through regular, built-in review and revision

- Link ongoing performance evaluation directly to concrete action steps

- Accelerate turnaround time and increase productivity

- Create a dynamic of ongoing results-oriented dialogue

The following best practices for coaching are all based on the FAST Feedback method. Learn them yourself, and teach other managers how to use them. A worksheet has been provided after these practices, to prepare you for giving FAST Feedback.

JUSTinTIME BEST PRACTICES
_ Coaching With _
FAST Feedback

1. Emphasize feedback itself. Teach managers to communicate with their people in a way that is directly responsive to the words and actions of those people.

2. Require managers to adjust the frequency of the feedback they give direct reports so that it's in tune with each contributor's unique needs. Remember, every employee has his or her own "feedback frequency." Different employees need different amounts and different types of feedback, and these factors are likely to vary over time.

Supervisory managers must think about each person who reports to them, evaluate how much feedback each person needs, and "tune in" to the feedback opportunities that work best in each individual case.

3. Insist that managers provide feedback that is correct, balanced, and appropriate. Every time a manager gives feedback to a direct report, the credibility of the manager—and of the entire organization—is on the line. That's why it's so important that managers check their facts before giving feedback, strike a healthy balance between praise and criticism, and always choose their words carefully.

4. Make sure managers understand that feedback is not specific enough unless it points to concrete action steps. Every instance of feedback is also an opportunity to delegate—that means assigning concrete goals and deadlines with clear parameters.

5. Expect managers to give feedback in a timely manner—as soon as possible after the performance in question. Immediate feedback makes the greatest impact. But timeliness requires good time management.

Initiate these best practices with the JUSTinTIME worksheet for preparing to give FAST Feedback.

WORKSHEET: FAST FEEDBACK PREPARATION

Directions: Select a contributor and an instance of perform-ance that requires FAST Feedback. Take time to prepare: Question your assumptions, check facts, balance praise and criticism, and delegate at least one goal with clear guidelines, parameters, and deadline. Then choose your words carefully: *Exactly what do you want to say, and how do you say it?*

Contributor:	
Instance of performance needing feedback:	
Question your assumptions about the matter.	**Are you sure?**
Check your facts about the matter.	**Are you sure?**

↪ **WORKSHEET:** FEEDBACK

Praise	Constructive Criticism

Tangible Goals	Deadlines	Parameters & Guidelines

REFINE THE MESSAGE

6.

JUST in TIME
Rewards
and Incentives

THERE IS AN OLD SAYING: "Managers get the performance they reward." If you want results, you have to reward results, and nothing else. The problem is that the old-fashioned incentives—long-term employment, steps up the organization's hierarchy, six-month reviews, annual raises, and standard benefits—are no longer enough to motivate the best talent. In the just-in-time workplace, you can't expect people to wait around to be rewarded once they've delivered—long-term rewards are out. People want to know what you have to offer them today, tomorrow, and next week in return for their added value. What is more, in order to drive the best performance in the workplace of the future, it is necessary to pay contributors not just in cold cash, but also in a wide range of currencies they value (financial and nonfinancial alike), remembering that different people value different currencies.

Managers need to reward desired performance consistently and with speed and creativity. Three factors should guide rewards and incentives in the workplace of the future:

1. Control
2. Timing
3. Customization

1. CONTROL

If the role of rewards is to drive performance, then managers should make performance the only lever for controlling rewards. That means it is critical to make very clear to individual contributors exactly what performance—what results, within what guidelines, parameters, and deadlines—the organization needs and will therefore reward. This must be done on an ongoing basis because the results required of any contributor in any organization nowadays are likely to be in constant flux.

Rewards should not be spread around equally in an effort to treat all contributors the same, unless business leaders are trying to turn their organizations into communes. The issue of fairness often comes up when a difference in pay for high performers is discussed, so let me offer a way to think about fairness. *There is nothing that is less fair than rewarding high performers and low performers the same.* Compensating high performers at a higher rate is not only fair, it's the *only fair way.* Rewards should not be wasted on people who fail to meet stated goals and deadlines. And individual contributors who perform must be made confident that their performance will result in proportionate financial and nonfinancial compensation. Every single resource an employer can make available to employees should be positioned as an incentive for performance.

Just as managers must become performance coaches, they must also position themselves as purchasing agents—purchasing the added value (concrete results) of individual contributors every day in exchange for compensation. And as purchasing agents must negotiate with vendors, managers must learn to negotiate with employees. Employees can be expected to drive a hard bargain, and so should managers. Much as it does with vendors, the market ultimately will dictate acceptable terms in each case.

2. TIMING

Reward people when they deliver results—no sooner, no later. Speed matters more than ever nowadays, so give people an incentive to perform quickly. That doesn't mean relaxing standards, but rather encouraging contributors to meet high performance standards as fast as they can. When contributors meet their goals within stated guidelines and parameters, managers should cash them out immediately and prepare to renegotiate. Immediate rewards are the most effective for three main reasons:

1. There can be no doubt about the reason for the rewards, providing a greater sense of control and a higher level of reinforcement.

2. Contributors are more likely to remember the precise details and context of the performance, and thus are better able to replicate the desired performance.

3. Contributors do not spend time wondering about whether their performance has been noted and appreciated, and so are less likely to lose the momentum generated by instances of success.

3. Customization

Managers often complain that today's employees are too demanding.

"This one wants Thursdays off."

"That one wants her own office."

"This one wants to bring his dog to work."

"That one wants to go to every training class we offer."

And so forth. But managers are wrong to complain. When a manager discovers the wants and needs of an individual contributor, the manager has found a needle in a haystack. Different people are motivated by very different incentives. Too often managers never find out exactly which rewards their individual employees want most and are therefore willing to work hardest to earn. In some cases, the desired rewards are so idiosyncratic, a manager wouldn't guess them in a million years if the employee didn't offer clues. And even when managers get the clues and find out what their employees want, they often regard the desired rewards as unreasonable or unrealistic.

A much better strategy is to use the discovery of desired rewards as an opportunity to motivate individual contributors with uniquely attractive incentives. Use the desired rewards as bargaining chips in the "purchasing agent" negotiation for added value.

> *"You want Thursdays off? I'm glad to know that. Here's what I need from you."*

> *"You want your own office? OK. Here's what I need from you."*

> *"You want to bring your dog to work? Great. Here's what I need from you."*

> *"You want to take advantage of our training classes? Here's what I need from you."*

Trade every customized incentive for concrete goals with clear guidelines, parameters, and deadlines.

The best practices that follow will help you establish JUSTinTIME rewards and incentives. Look closely at these practices and begin putting them into action with the brainstorming exercises and handy worksheet that round out this chapter.

JUSTinTIME Best Practices
— Rewards & Incentives —

1. Make a short-term pay-for-performance deal with every employee on every project. Pay for results delivered by specific deadlines, instead of by the hour, and cash out employees when they deliver.

2. Go beyond salaries, hourly wages, and the traditional benefits by expanding your repertoire of financial rewards. Move toward a higher and higher ratio of variable performance-based compensation versus fixed compensation. Consider additional incentive features such as on-the-spot cash awards and, in appropriate circumstances, equity. Offer customizable pension and health benefits that allow each employee to make decisions about desired coverage, relative cost-effectiveness, and portability.

Any serious overhaul of the compensation system will require a thorough appraisal and forward-thinking leadership on the part of the organization's financial officers and compensation team.

 Position quasi-financial benefits as part of your compensation plan. Quasi-financials include concierge services (such as dry-cleaning, gift delivery, and grocery shopping); wellness services (such as athletic club memberships, yoga classes, and massage treatments); and family support (ranging from child-care to elder-care).

4. Include pure nonfinancial rewards in your compensation plan. Our research reveals six nonfinancial rewards that are most sought by the workforce of the future:

- Control over one's work schedule
- Training opportunities
- Exposure to decision-makers
- Personal credit for tangible results achieved
- Increased responsibility
- The chance for creative expression

These nonfinancial incentives should be administered as compensation elements and tied to performance just as financial rewards are.

5. Empower managers on the front lines. To reward high performers rapidly, consistently, and creatively, managers on the front lines require greater resources and discretion with their direct reports.

The short-term adjustment that can be made quickly and with relative ease is (a) to identify all elements of the current compensation system that are potentially variable, and get managers to start using them; and (b) to mobilize additional financial resources that managers can utilize to achieve a greater ratio of variable rewards.

> *Initiate these best practices with*
> *the JUSTinTIME exercises and worksheet*
> *for rewards and incentives.*

Brainstorming
Exercises — Rewards and Incentives

A. EVALUATION

Purpose: To evaluate your current rewards and incentives situation.

Please answer the following questions:

1. What is the basis of most compensation in your organization (or team)?

Salary and/or hourly pay?
Or pay for results delivered by specific deadlines?

2. In what currencies are contributions in your organization (or team) compensated?

Money and standard benefits?
Or every possible financial and nonfinancial resource that can be positioned as an incentive?

3. What behavior is rewarded more in your organization (or team)?

Putting in time?
Or delivering results?

4. How does one become highly remunerated in your organization (or team)?

➔ *Brainstorming Exercises*

By achieving seniority?
Or by demonstrating speed, quality, innovation, and self-management?

5. When (how often) are contributors in your organization (or team) rewarded?

   Payments at regular intervals, and raises and bonuses annually, semiannually, quarterly, or monthly?
   Or on an ongoing basis whenever they deliver results?

6. Do managers on the front lines have sufficient discretionary resources—financial and non-financial—to play the role of purchasing agents in day-to-day negotiations with individual contributors?

7. What elements of your current compensation are currently available?

   What performance-based incentives (raises, bonuses, promotions, other financials and nonfinancials) can be awarded?

8. Do managers in your organization (or team) take full advantage of existing opportunities to reward high performers? If not, what can be done to encourage and support the full use of existing performance incentives?

➔ *Brainstorming Exercises*

9. What opportunities do employees have to customize benefits based on their own particular needs when it comes to desired coverage, relative cost-effectiveness, and portability?

B. INVENTORY: FINANCIAL REWARDS

Purpose: To inventory all of the latent resources available in your organization (or team) that could be mobilized and positioned as financial incentives for day-to-day performance.

FINANCIAL REWARDS

Currently Available (Mark with an asterisk the rewards now positioned as performance-based rewards.)

Additional resources that could be made available to managers as performance-based awards:

➤ *Brainstorming Exercises*

C. INVENTORY: QUASI-FINANCIAL REWARDS

Purpose: To inventory all latent resources available in your organization (or team).

QUASI-FINANCIAL REWARDS

Currently Available (Mark with an asterisk the rewards now positioned as performance-based rewards.)
CONCIERGE SERVICES
WELLNESS SERVICES
FAMILY SUPPORT SERVICES

➔ *Brainstorming Exercises*

QUASI-FINANCIAL REWARDS (cont.)

Additional resources that could be made available as performance-based rewards:

CONCIERGE SERVICES

WELLNESS SERVICES

FAMILY SUPPORT SERVICES

➤ *Brainstorming Exercises*

D. INVENTORY: NONFINANCIAL REWARDS

Purpose: To inventory all latent resources available in your organization (or team).

PURE NONFINANCIAL REWARDS

	Currently Available (Mark with an asterisk rewards now positioned as performance-based rewards.)	Additional Resources that could be made available as performance-based rewards.
Increased control over one's work schedule		
Chances for training and learning		
Exposure to decision-makers		

➔ *Brainstorming Exercises*

PURE NONFINANCIAL REWARDS (Cont.)

	Currently Available (Mark with an asterisk rewards now positioned as performance-based rewards.)	Additional Resources that could be made available as performance-based rewards.
Personal credit for tangible results achieved		
Increased responsib- ility		
Chances for creative expression		

CONCLUDED

WORKSHEET: PERFORMANCE AGREEMENTS

Directions: Use this worksheet to arrange short-term pay for performance agreements.

Individual Contributor:

Manager:

Date of Agreement:

Goal:	FINANCIAL REWARDS	NONFINANCIAL REWARDS
Deadline:		
Guidelines and Parameters:		

➤ WORKSHEET: Performance Agreements

Guidelines and Parameters:	FINANCIAL REWARDS	NONFINANCIAL REWARDS

JUST in TIME
Retention

IN TODAY'S TIGHT LABOR MARKET, business leaders agonize about high turnover because so many employees come and go before they deliver a decent return on the organization's recruiting and training investment. That's why retention will remain the number one concern of human resource professionals for the foreseeable future. In addressing this concern, though, we must remember the answer to this pocket guide's initial question: "How do you get the best people to pay their dues and climb the ladder in the old-fashioned way?" **YOU DON'T.** A corollary to that question is, "How do you retain people long-term as exclusive, full-time, on-site, employees with uninterrupted service?" *Once again, the answer is* **YOU DON'T.**

Too many business leaders and managers think of retention in terms of those kinds of questions, and as long as they do, they won't have a chance of solving the turnover problem. Moreover, if an organization has only one way of retaining people, then it has only one way of getting a return on its recruiting and training investment. And that is just bad business.

So what is the *right* question to ask? It's *"How do you maintain good working relationships with the best people throughout their working lives?"*

You don't have to retain people long-term as exclusive, full-time, on-site employees with uninterrupted service. In fact, if you did, you would find your organization overly constrained by rigid employment relationships. Nowadays, the best way to get the best work out of the best people consistently is to take the "as-needed" approach: on-again, off-again; sometimes full-time, sometimes flex-time, sometimes part-time; sometimes on-site, sometimes off-site; sometimes on an exclusive basis, and sometimes as a shared resource. It doesn't matter where, when, or how you get the best people to contribute the most work at the highest levels of speed and accuracy, as long as you get them to make those contributions when you need them.

The key to retention is to redefine retention so that it means "access to the talent you need when you need it." With that redefinition, the way to retain talent is to stay lean and learn to thrive on short-term flexible employment relationships with the best free-agent employees. The best people who serve you well on

a consistent basis will be your new lifelong employees. Retain the best people one at a time, one day
at a time, on the basis of an ongoing negotiation with
each individual on his or her own unique terms.

If you are willing to negotiate in order to retain, then
you can transform the reasons why the best people
leave into the reasons why the best people will stay.
According to our research, there are five reasons why
people typically leave their jobs nowadays (apart
from a huge differential in pay opportunity):

1. **Relationships.** In the majority of cases, peo-
    ple leave their job because they are unhappy
    with their boss or manager, further reinforcing
    the importance of the manager–direct-report
    relationship.

    The best way to deal with this factor is to take
    preventive measures—making sure that super-
    visory managers play the role of performance
    coach (see Chapter 5). When preventive mea-
    sures fail, the challenge is to move the employee
    into the supervisory orbit of another manager
    without losing the employee altogether.

    It is important to note, however, that an employ-
    ee's relationship with his or her manager/boss
    is not the only relationship that may influence
    whether that employee leaves or stays. Other

relationships with a powerful impact include those with co-workers, subordinates, vendors, and clients or customers.

By working to improve problem relationships, or by moving contributors out of such relationships and into new ones, many unnecessary turnovers can be prevented.

2. **Schedule.** This is almost as big a factor as relationships. Sometimes people want to work more, sometimes they want to work less; often they simply want to work the same hours but on flex-time or compressed-time. In many cases, even a slight adjustment in a person's schedule will be enough to make that person leave or stay (see Chapter 4).

3. **Work.** Often people leave because they want to tackle new challenges—new tasks, responsibilities, or projects—that they feel will not be available to them if they remain in the same job or working in the same organization. If they can find those new challenges in the same job or, at least, the same organization, often they *will* stay (again, see Chapter 4).

4. **Skills.** In today's world, where it is critical to keep building one's skills faster than they become obsolete, individuals—especially the

best, most skilled individuals—feel a strong compulsion to be learning all the time. Thus when people feel they have exhausted the learning opportunities in an organization, they often leave in search of new ones. As long as such employees are learning voraciously on the job, though, they are unlikely to leave.

The challenge for employers is to maintain an environment of constant voracious learning. That doesn't always mean offering formal training programs or giving financial support for external education. Often it means creating an infrastructure of learning resources and a culture of knowledge work (see Chapter 3).

5. **Location.** Sometimes people want or need to work in a different place because of a change in their life's circumstances. That different place might be a certain city, town, county, or state, or even a particular country. In such a case, an employer may not have the ability to accommodate the want or need; but many employers do. When an organization is geographically widespread, all it takes is a transfer.

Of course, employee transfers present many issues, not least of which is that the transferring manager will still lose a valued employee. However, if the complicating factors can be worked out, at least the organization as a whole will retain an employee who would otherwise be lost altogether.

It should be noted that the desire to work in a new location could simply mean a desire to work at home some or all of the time. Whenever practical, retaining the employee as a telecommuter is preferable to losing the employee (see Chapter 4).

Remember: the factors that prompt valuable contributors to leave can often be transformed into factors that make valuable contributors stay, if an employer is willing to negotiate. Indeed it is often an employer's willingness to negotiate and, ultimately, accommodate on such matters that can make an otherwise ordinary employment relationship uniquely valuable to an individual contributor. The strong likelihood is that long-term employment relationships in the workplace of the future will be based on how well the work situation fits each individual contributor's unique life plan (not the reverse).

The following best practices will help you initiate JUSTinTIME retention. A brainstorming exercise has been included after those practices, along with a useful worksheet for personal retention planning.

JUSTinTIME Best Practices
— Retention —

1. Develop personal retention plans from day one. Don't wait until an employee is considering leaving to ask, "Is there anything we can do to keep you?" Ask on the first day of employment, and keep asking every single day.

- What changing role might your organization play in the career of each new hire as he or she moves from one stage of life to the next?

- What changing roles might each new hire play in the future of the organization?

- What might you have to offer each other as the employer-employee relationship grows and evolves over time?

If you begin this dialogue on day one, it is much more likely to survive over time and make a difference at key turning points down the road, when an employee is likely to question his or her work situation.

2. Provide internal "escape hatches" so people can reinvent themselves, their roles, their careers, and their circumstances without leaving the organization. Provide people with opportunities to relocate geographically, to enter new skill areas, to work with new people, to take on new tasks and responsibilities, and to work new schedules.

3. Encourage people to "leave without leaving." Once the organization has invested in recruiting and training a person, management has a stake in retaining that person—even if not as a full-time on-site employee. If you can't keep the whole employee, why not keep as much of the employee as you can? Instead of losing valued people, offer them the chance to work part-time or flex-time. See if they are interested in working as telecommuters, periodic temps, or consultants. And offer unpaid sabbaticals.

4. Build a "reserve army." When valued people do leave, consider them part of your reserve army. Stay in touch with them. Put them in your proprietary talent database (see Chapter 2). Call them up for active duty when there is a project that fits. Try re-recruiting them after they've had a chance to see the grass isn't so much greener on the other side.

> *Initiate these best practices with the JUSTinTIME exercise and and worksheet for retention.*

Brainstorming
Exercise — Retention

RETENTION EVALUATION

Purpose: To evaluate your current retention situation.

Please answer the following questions:

1. What is the current turnover rate in your organization (or team)?

2. Do you consider this high?

3. Is turnover causing a staffing problem in your organization (or team)? If yes, then please take a moment to articulate that problem. How would you describe it?

   • As an inability to get all of the work done?

   • As a drain because of the ongoing recruiting and training of new people?

   • As an insufficient return on the recruiting and training investment?

   • As too much pressure on remaining staff to fill in the gaps?

   As all or some of the above?
   As something else?

4. What is the current approach to retention in your organization (or team)?

→ *Brainstorming Exercises*

- Full-time, or not necessarily full-time?

- On-site, or not necessarily on-site?

- Uninterrupted, or not necessarily uninterrupted?

- Exclusive, or not necessarily exclusive?

5. How would you describe the career paths in your organization?

    - One size fits all?

    - Several paths to achieve the top level of success?

    - Many paths to achieve the top level of success?

    - As many paths as there are people, all leading potentially to the top level?

6. Do managers and leaders in your organization (or team) engage in career-planning dialogues with valued contributors? If yes, then what do they talk about?

7. How much flexibility do managers have to negotiate with and accommodate valued contributors on issues that make an impact on retention?

    For example, how much flexibility do they

→ *Brainstorming Exercises*

have with issues such as:

- Relationships?
- Schedule?
- Work?
- Skills?
- Location?

8. What happens in your organization (or team) when a valued employee leaves?

- Is that person never welcome to return?
- If the person returns, does he or she have to start all over again?
- If the person returns, does the person start where he or she left off?

Are former employees actively re-recruited in hopes that they will return?

Are former employees called on an as-needed basis to fill in where needed?

CONCLUDED

*Now begin your
JUSTinTIME retention planning
with the following worksheet.*

WORKSHEET: RETENTION PLANNING

Directions: Use this planning worksheet as needed to make adjustments in the roles of valued contributors.

Name:

FACTOR	CURRENT ROLE	POSSIBLE ADJUSTMENTS
Relation-ships		
Schedule		

➔ WORKSHEET: RETENTION

FACTOR	CURRENT ROLE	POSSIBLE ADJUSTMENTS
Tasks		
Skill Development		
Location		

One Last JUSTinTIME Review

AS WE HAVE SEEN IN THIS POCKET GUIDE, JUSTinTIME Leadership is about staying lean and flexible in the post-industrial age, maintaining access to the talent you need, and maximizing that talent on an as-needed basis. The systems and practices in this pocket guide are designed to help managers and leaders get the best work out of the best people consistently—wherever, whenever, and however those people can add value.

The underlying assumption of JUSTinTIME Leadership is that, in the new economy, organizations will have to move beyond the static long-term staffing models toward a more fluid model. This approach is supported by best practices that give leaders and managers the advantage when it comes to maximizing human talent in the new economy. The benefits of these practices include human resources that grow at desired levels without compromising productivity; an improved return on recruiting and training investments; the ability to seize, first and fast, new market opportunities as they emerge; and a dynamic corporate culture that promotes innovation.

The JUSTinTIME Leadership pocket guide has focused on six main areas: staffing, training, performance management, coaching with FAST Feedback, rewards and incentives, and retention. Let's take one last look at the best practices in each area, focusing on the most essential points of those practices.

BEST PRACTICES

JUSTinTIME Staffing

1. Shrink your core group, and retool your organization so it can thrive with a very small number of full-time, long-term, on-site employees.

2. Grow your fluid talent pool. Reorganize as much day-to-day work as possible so it can be done by that pool's talent—relatively short-term employees working in flexible arrangements.

3. Build a proprietary talent database of individual contributors whom you can call upon for temporary help as needed. Index the database by key skill and performance criteria.

4. Develop solid working relationships with a wide range of vendors who can be counted upon for outsourcing.

5. Maintain an internal group of contributors who are not permanently assigned to any particular tasks/responsibilities, teams, locations, or schedules, and who can be called upon and deployed to fill in staffing gaps wherever and whenever they occur.

JUSTinTIME Training

1. Gear the training of individual contributors for the specific tasks, responsibilities, and projects on which they will be working in the very near term.

2. Get new contributors up to speed very quickly so they can start adding value right away.

3. Create a just-in-time training infrastructure with maximum information resources in many different media in order to support ongoing as-needed learning.

4. Transform your corporate culture by making everybody a knowledge worker. Help every contributor leverage information, skill, and knowledge to accomplish every task and responsibility.

JUSTinTIME
Performance Management

1. Pull together teams based on who has the skills to fill the roles necessary to achieve clear goals with concrete deadlines, and require them to disband when their mission is completed.

2. Assign every tangible result to an owner, attach a concrete deadline to every tangible result, and spell out all the parameters, guidelines, and specifications up front.

3. For longer-term projects, require result-owners to create and submit plans of action, including intermediate goals and deadlines along with action steps for achieving those goals.

4. Advise individual contributors in the basics of self-management.

5. Keep performance evaluation brief, straight, simple, and tied directly to measuring the achievement of goals and deadlines.

6. Manage results instead of time. As long as individual contributors are delivering results, forget about time altogether.

JUSTinTIME Coaching:
The FAST Feedback Method

1. Teach managers to communicate with the people they manage in a way that is directly responsive to the words and actions of those people.

2. Require managers to adjust the frequency of the feedback they give direct reports so it's in tune with each contributor's unique needs.

3. Insist that managers provide feedback that is correct, balanced, and appropriate.

4. Make sure managers understand that every instance of feedback is also an opportunity to delegate—that means assigning concrete goals and deadlines with clear parameters.

5. Expect managers to give feedback in a timely manner—as soon as possible after the performance in question.

JUSTinTIME
Rewards and Incentives

1. Pay for results delivered by specific deadlines, instead of by the hour, and cash out employees when they deliver.

2. Go beyond salaries, hourly wages, and traditional benefits by expanding your repertoire of financial rewards. Move toward a higher and higher ratio of variable performance-based compensation versus fixed compensation.

3. Position quasi-financial benefits as part of your compensation plan.

4. Include pure nonfinancial rewards in your compensation plan.

5. Empower managers on the front lines. To reward high performers rapidly, consistently, and creatively, managers on the front lines require greater resources and discretion with their direct reports.

JUSTinTIME Retention

1. Develop personal retention plans from day one. Don't wait until an employee is considering leaving to ask, "Is there anything we can do to keep you?" Ask on the first day of employment, and keep asking every single day.

2. Provide individual contributors with opportunities to relocate geographically, to enter new skill areas, to work with new people, to take on new tasks and responsibilities, and to work new schedules.

3. Once the organization has invested in recruiting and training a person, retain as much of the person as you can. Offer valued employees the chance to work part-time or flex-time. See if they are interested in working as telecommuters, periodic temps, or consultants. And offer unpaid sabbaticals.

4. When valued people do leave, put them in your proprietary talent database and consider them part of your "reserve army."

IN CONCLUSION

I hope you found the JUSTinTIME Leadership pocket guide to be clear, simple, and practical. It is my greatest hope that you will be able to apply these ideas and best practices to the issues you face every day in the real world with your organization or team. As I mentioned in the introduction, when you start doing things differently in your sphere of control, your team will begin to show dramatic improvements in productivity, morale, and retention. That's when your actions will be recognized as bold and innovative leadership.

Again, I wish you the best of luck in becoming a change leader wherever this pocket guide finds you working.